YOU CAN'T BE TIMID WITH A
TRUMPET *Notes from the Orchestra*

YOU CAN'T BE TIMID WITH A TRUMPET

Notes from the Orchestra

BETTY LOU ENGLISH

Drawings by Stan Skardinski

Lothrop, Lee & Shepard Books • New York

ACKNOWLEDGMENTS

Many generous people helped to make this book. I am grateful to Susan Kagan, Adjunct Lecturer in Music, Hunter College, New York, who introduced me to a number of the musicians in the book; to Eugene King, music teacher, Fieldston Lower School, New York, who supplied several very useful references; and to Betsy Wade Boylan, newspaper editor, for her wit and wisdom.

My sincere thanks, also, to Mortimer H. Frank, Professor of English, Bronx Community College, City University of New York and Contributing Editor to *Fanfare* magazine, who gave me research materials and many excellent suggestions as well.

I am especially indebted to Martin Bernstein, musicologist and Professor Emeritus, Graduate School of Arts and Sciences, New York University, who read the manuscript and patiently answered my many questions.

And, of course, I particularly want to thank all of the musicians in the book who gave their time and interest so liberally to this project.

Library of Congress Cataloging in Publication Data. English, Betty Lou. You can't be timid with a trumpet. Summary: A conductor and seventeen men and women from nine well-known orchestras discuss their relationship with music and their individual instruments. 1. Musicians—United States—Biography—Juvenile literature. [1. Musicians. 2. Orchestra] I. Skardinski, Stan. II. Title. ML3930.A2E53 785'.092'2 [920] 80-13348 ISBN 0-688-41963-1 ISBN 0-688-51963-6 (lib. bdg.)

FOR A.L.L.

CONTENTS

INTRODUCTION

The symphony orchestra as we know it today consists of four main groups of instruments—strings, woodwinds, brass, and percussion—as well as the harp and several keyboard instruments. To make this large group of finely crafted instruments produce the music of the great composers requires about one hundred highly trained and talented players and one conductor.

In the following pages we'll meet seventeen of these men and women, selected from eight different well-known orchestras and representing the seventeen major orchestral instruments. Also included is a conductor, who is responsible for making the instrumentalists' individually created sounds come together as he or she understands the composer intended.

As each musician talks about his or her instrument we gain a sense of its special character. The stories of these people also show us some of the struggles and rewards of the professional musician's life. Their experiences are sometimes humorous, sometimes nearly disastrous. But most striking is the impression they give us of each musician's intense commitment to his or her instrument and to music itself.

Cleveland Orchestra in rehearsal.

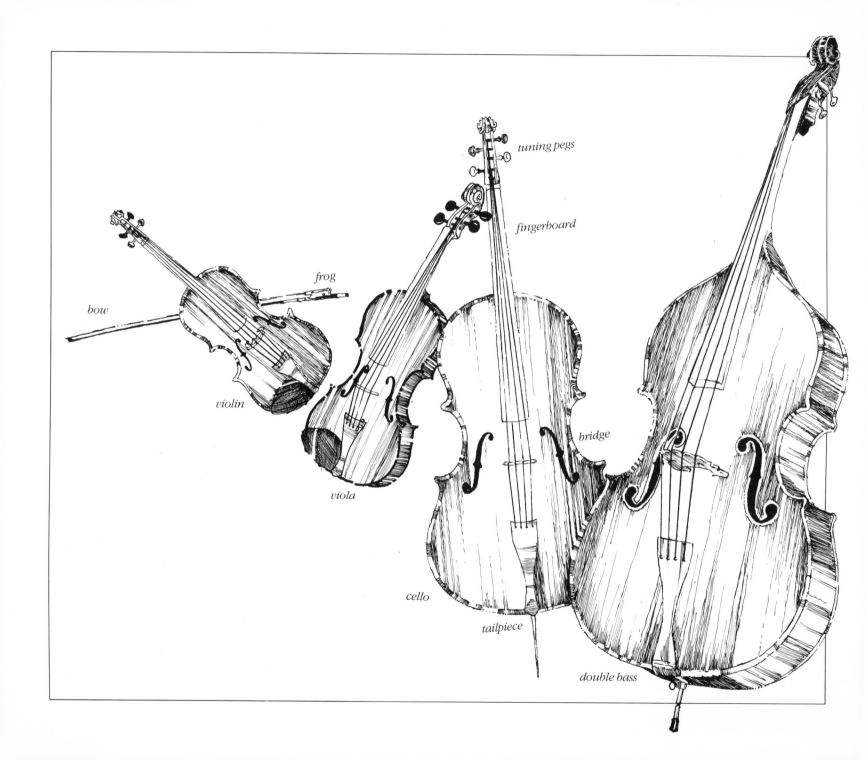

tuning pegs

fingerboard

frog

bow

violin

viola

cello

bridge

tailpiece

double bass

STRINGS

The violin, viola, cello, and double bass are all made of wood and all have four strings—some wire, some sheep gut, some gut wrapped with wire—that are stretched from the tailpiece over the bridge and along the length of the fingerboard to be wound around the tuning pegs. While the fingers of the player's left hand press the strings against the fingerboard, so altering their vibrating length and consequently their sound, the right hand holds the bow. The horse-tail hair stretched from the tip of the bow to the frog—the part the player holds—makes the strings sound when it is drawn across them. The hollow wooden body of the instrument makes the sound stronger. Sometimes, instead of bowing, the musician plucks the strings with his finger.

While the violin and viola go back hundreds of years, in their present form they were perfected in the eighteenth century by such Italian craftsmen as Stradivarius and members of the Guarneri and Amati families. The modern cello dates from the middle of the seventeenth century and the double bass originated in the sixteenth century.

SAMUEL MAGAD

Co-Concertmaster, Chicago Symphony Orchestra

The excitement of the occasion was so great that I wasn't nervous at all when, at eleven years old, I played the Mendelssohn Violin Concerto with the Chicago Symphony Orchestra. Nor, of course, did I have any idea that many years later I would become co-concertmaster of that same orchestra.

Because my father was a violinist, the sound of the violin was part of my life from the very beginning, and I started to take lessons when I was five. I had such a love of music and such a strong desire to play that I learned quickly and so was invited to perform that concerto with the Chicago Symphony when I was still quite young. It was a good many years later, after studying music at De Paul University and then playing in the Army orchestra in Washington, that I auditioned for the Chicago Symphony. I've been with the orchestra ever since and became co-concertmaster in 1972.

As concertmaster, the principal violinist in the orchestra, I have some special duties. Tuning the orchestra is one of them. I ask the oboist to play an A so that all the other musicians can tune to that note. Another part of my job is to help the other violinists understand the way the conductor interprets the music. For instance, I set the bowing patterns that will produce the effects the conductor wants. Playing the solo violin parts that sometimes appear in orchestral music and performing with the Chicago Symphony Chamber Players are the most difficult but also the most pleasurable parts of being

concertmaster. When I'm not busy with orchestra rehearsals and performances, and of course with practicing, I teach at Northwestern University and play in the resident string quartet there.

Part of the excitement of being with a major orchestra is touring. We play all over the United States and in other parts of the world as well. Once when we were in Edinburgh, Scotland, I had changed at the hotel into the full dress suit, tails and all, that I would wear in the performance at the nearby concert hall. My wife was wearing a long formal gown. As we walked out of the hotel we were greeted by a cheering crowd. You can imagine our confusion–until we discovered that we had been mistaken for Princess Marguerite of Denmark and her husband, who were also staying at the hotel.

For me, the violin has the most beautiful sound of all the string instruments. It's the soprano of the string family and has a lyrical, singing quality. The most versatile of all the strings, it can produce a great variety of tone colors. And the variety of music written for it is unlimited. Playing this music and hearing it performed at the highest level, as it is in our orchestra, well, that's worth all my hours of practice.

EDWARD ORMOND

Assistant Principal Viola, Cleveland Orchestra

When I was seven years old, my father took me to a violin recital and I fell in love with the sound, and I said, "Papa, buy me one of those." All I wanted was to learn to play the violin, but my father warned me that it was a difficult life and he was reluctant for me to take up the instrument. It wasn't until four years later that a relative gave me a violin, and my father couldn't resist my enthusiasm any longer. I became engrossed with everything about music, read books about composers, and practiced three or four hours a day. But of course I still found time for football and baseball. And although I was looked upon as the "violin virtuoso," the neighborhood tough, who loved my violin playing, protected me and wouldn't let anybody call me "sissy" for what I was doing.

Usually a musician continues with the instrument he starts with, but for me it was different. When it was time for college, I started at New York University, then transferred to the University of Michigan, and found that they needed a violist in their orchestra. I had already been playing the viola as well as the violin. Although the viola is a little larger than the violin, the two instruments are played so similarly that a violinist can become a violist very easily and I actually auditioned on both instruments for summer study at Tanglewood. While for some people the viola is too large to handle comfortably, for me it was the ideal size and it became my instrument. It may lack the brilliance of the violin, but its warm, mellow quality appeals very much to my ear.

There is a great thrill in being in the middle of a musical construction. I feel this particularly when playing string quartets since the viola is the center or middle voice of the string family, below the first and second violins at the top and above the cello at the bottom. Among all the wonderful quartets, perhaps the Beethoven quartets are my favorites. In quartet playing, each instrument has an important line, not merely an accompaniment to the first violin, so that the four players have to figure out when each instrument should be brought forward as the music moves along. I love that challenge and I love the depth of feeling in the music–its strength and gentleness. Playing it on my Amati viola is a special experience. Some of the finest violas were made by members of the Amati family who lived in Cremona, Italy, in the sixteenth and seventeenth centuries. Mine was made in 1619.

During the time that I was studying for my master's degree at the University of Michigan and at Juilliard, I took off one year and played in the Indianapolis Orchestra for two seasons. Later I became assistant principal violist with the St. Louis Symphony Orchestra before moving to that same position with the Cleveland Orchestra. I remember that at my first orchestral performance, even though I had practiced with a diligence that's never been matched since, I was scared stiff. And now, although I've been playing in orchestras for thirty-two years, I may not be scared stiff anymore but I'm still just as excited as I was when I started.

GERALD KAGAN

Assistant Principal Cello, Metropolitan Opera Orchestra

Someone said to the conductor of my junior high school orchestra, "He's a big kid; why don't you give him a cello to play?" I thought that would be fun and it turned out it was, probably because I love the sound of the singing voice, and the cello's sound is so similar to it. It's closest to the tenor, but the cello's range is much greater, and its dark tonal quality is especially appealing to me.

When I was given a scholarship to the Juilliard School of Music in New York, I studied with Leonard Rose, a wonderful man and a wonderful teacher. One of the exercises he gave me was to play the same scale five hours a day for a week. Repeating the same scale over and over left me free to concentrate on correct bowing technique, the most difficult part of playing the cello. In order for the fingers to feel the relationship between the bow and the strings, the bow must be held correctly. It's the fingers moving from the knuckles, plus the suppleness of the wrist, that enables the player to operate the bow correctly. The wrist and fingers, guided by the arm, determine the volume, quality, and variety of the sound. But to beginning students, the bow feels much heavier than its two and one-half ounces and, as a result, they tend to compensate by letting the arm do the work of the wrist and fingers.

My cello is quite special. I bought it from a collector who had discovered it in a pawn shop in Portugal. It was two hundred years old and had been made by Leopold Ren-

audin in Paris. It needed extensive restoration, but the collector despaired of having it done because it was so costly, and so he sold it to me and I restored it myself. The raised gold letters around all the ribs form the Latin words *Ego sum anima musicae* ("I am the spirit of music") then the initials J.G. and the Roman numerals MDXXXVI (1536). What is the meaning of the initials and the date? I've discovered that there was a man named Granier who lived in the sixteenth century and who was a virtuoso on the viola da gamba, the forerunner of the cello. He also played the double bass and had his instrument fixed so that a child could be concealed inside and sing while Granier performed on the instrument. He was well-known for this stunt, but none of the references I've found give him a first name. In old biographical dictionaries he's always referred to as "a certain Granier." Was his first initial J., and could he have been born in 1536? Was he the J.G. whose initials were so carefully embossed on this cello in the 1780s, some two hundred years after Granier's time? I still haven't solved the mystery.

After graduating from Juilliard, I auditioned for the St. Louis Symphony. I was to play for the orchestra's representative in New York, but there was a big party going on in the apartment where he was staying, so we went to find a quieter place. We wound up in a tailor's shop, where I played above the noise of one of those steam-compression pressing machines. But I got the job anyway.

I was with the Pittsburgh Symphony a few years later when a friend told me there was an opening in the Metropolitan Opera Orchestra. I've been here seventeen years now. Great singing is more exciting to me than symphonic music, and here I am, playing the instrument I love and listening to the greatest voices in the world almost every night of my life.

JON DEAK

Assistant Principal Double Bass, New York Philharmonic

It's not easy to travel with a double bass. Sometimes when I get to the boarding area at the airport, the airline's official looks at me and my bass and says, "My gosh, you can't take that on the plane." Of course they do let me take it on, but I have to buy a seat for it—sometimes even first-class.

I started playing the double bass, or bass as it is commonly called, in high school in Oak Park, Illinois. Having gone through a period of being interested in golf and wrestling, I began thinking about playing in the school orchestra. When I asked what instrument was needed, the conductor said basses. Soon I found that I liked the warm sound of the bass. It seems to me that musicians tend to talk like their instruments—people say that I mumble.

While I was in the school orchestra, I was also playing in a jazz band. I still like jazz, but classical music is more important to me. After studying at Oberlin College, and then the Juilliard School, I went to teach at the Interlochen Arts Academy in Michigan. I lived in a cabin in the wilderness near the lake. It was so cold that I could walk to work across the ice on the lake.

Later, when I was studying and teaching at the University of Illinois, I heard about an opening for a bass in the New York Philharmonic. The auditions lasted for three days because there were forty-nine others besides me. That was ten years ago and I've been

with the Philharmonic ever since. My first concert was in Central Park at night. Right in the middle of Beethoven's Third Piano Concerto the lights suddenly went out. We were in total darkness, couldn't see the music, and I thought, "Now what's going to happen?" But the musicians went right on playing and completed the piece in the dark.

Composing music is very important to me, and I spend a lot of time at it. I like to perform my own compositions and the works of other contemporary composers, but my six-year-old son likes it best when I play my one-man band. This is a contraption I've built that combines a bass, a harmonica, a melodica, and percussion instruments. I can play with my hands, feet, and mouth all at the same time.

The bass is a very flexible instrument; you can bow it, pluck it, rap it. You can even get it to make animal sounds. But it's only in the past twenty years that its possibilities have begun to be explored. The name "double bass," given to it long ago, describes the instrument's main function, which is to double the bass line (extend the range an octave lower) of the orchestra chords.

My bass is almost 250 years old. When I was in high school I worked for a man who repaired instruments. He had a bass. It was old and the wood was cracked, but he kept telling me what a great instrument it was. He fixed it and said that I could buy it. It was very expensive, however, and I didn't think that I could afford it, but my parents helped me out because they wanted me to have a good instrument.

Because the bass is so large, people like to make jokes about it. They say, "Don't you wish you'd taken up the piccolo?" or, "Bet you can't get that under your chin." Sometimes when people tease me like that, I knock on the bass and say, "Herman, are you in there? Are you all right?"

WOODWINDS

The sound of a woodwind instrument is produced by causing the column of air enclosed in it to vibrate. In the flute this happens when the player blows across the hole near the end of the silver instrument. With the reed instruments–the clarinet and bass clarinet have a single reed; the oboe, English horn, and bassoon have a double reed–the player blows through the reeds, which are made of thin pieces of cane. The tension of the reed and the length of the air column determine the pitch of the sound. Opening and closing the holes along the sides of the instruments by means of complicated systems of keys, plates, and levers changes the length of the air column.

The key system for the flute was invented by Theobald Boehm, a German flutist, in 1832. This improved the quality and tonal correctness of its sound and gave us the flute as we know it today. While the other woodwinds are not at all like the flute in appearance, three of them, the oboe, the English horn, and the clarinet, are visually very similar to each other. Made of rosewood, the oboe (from the French *hautbois*, "high wood,") was created in the mid-seventeenth century by the Frenchman Jean Hotteterre. Its interior shape, called the bore, becomes gradually wider from the mouthpiece to the bell. Two very thin pieces of cane bound together make its double reed. The English horn has a larger double reed, is longer than the oboe, and has a pear-shaped bell. The single-reed clarinet is made of ebonite and is cylindrical except for the bell. It was developed by Johann Denner, a Nuremberg instrument maker, at the end of the eighteenth century.

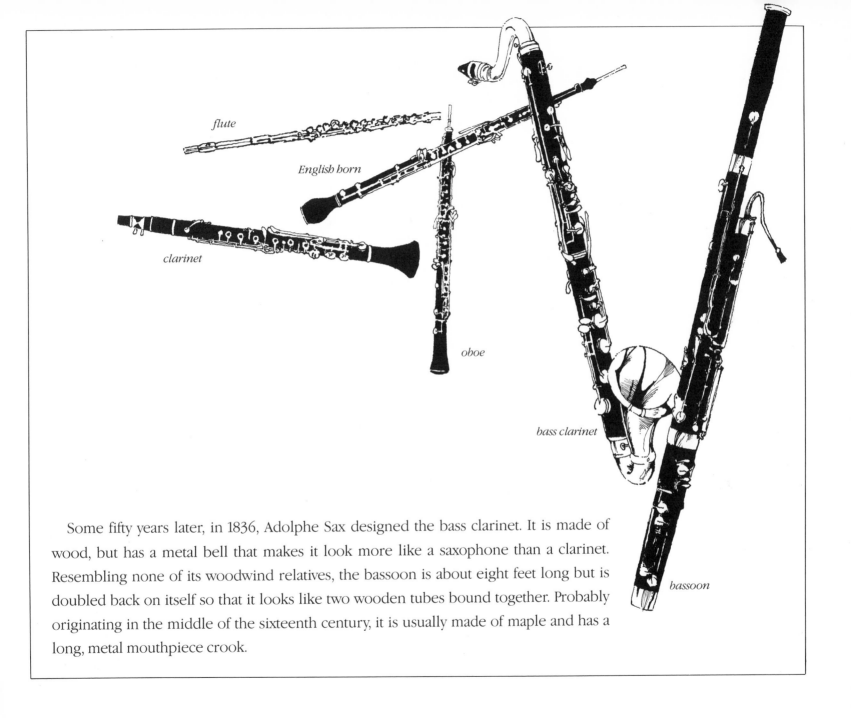

flute

English horn

clarinet

oboe

bass clarinet

bassoon

Some fifty years later, in 1836, Adolphe Sax designed the bass clarinet. It is made of wood, but has a metal bell that makes it look more like a saxophone than a clarinet. Resembling none of its woodwind relatives, the bassoon is about eight feet long but is doubled back on itself so that it looks like two wooden tubes bound together. Probably originating in the middle of the sixteenth century, it is usually made of maple and has a long, metal mouthpiece crook.

DORIOT ANTHONY DWYER

Principal Flute, Boston Symphony Orchestra

It was raining, the trees and bushes heavy with wet green leaves, when I got to Tanglewood to audition for principal flute of the Boston Symphony Orchestra. Since I had come from southern California, a desert climate where the sun nearly always shines, I thought the rain and brightness of the green were beautiful and inspiring. For two months I had been up many nights, coming home from playing concerts and then practicing for hours for what turned out to be a long and difficult audition. When I returned to California, where I was playing second flute with the Los Angeles Philharmonic, weeks went by without any word from Boston. Finally their manager called and offered me the job. There was a lot of excitement because this was the first time a woman had been appointed permanently for a principal position in a major symphony orchestra.

But in my family there are examples of what seem to me to be more unusual women. Susan B. Anthony, remembered for her fight to give women the vote, among many other rights, was my great-cousin. And my mother, who achieved artistry as a professional flutist, supported herself this way before she married–quite uncommon in those days. Mother was my first teacher, starting me as soon as I could hold the flute properly, which was when I was about eight. At first the progress was slow and very difficult, partly because I couldn't understand my mother's strictness, which was necessary to learn the three R's of music—reading, rhythm, and 'rithmetic—and also because music did not yet have any clear meaning to me, even though for years she had sat me down in front of the radio to listen to programs of symphony and opera performances with her. Finally, however, when we went to a Chicago Symphony Orchestra concert—I remember they played the *William Tell* Overture by Rossini—suddenly I understood what music was about, and it thrilled me.

When my parents saw my enthusiasm, they took me backstage to meet the first flutist, Ernest Liegl, and soon arrangements were made for me to study with him. I was so in awe of him I decided I must be perfect or he would not keep me as a student. Yes, I was nervous but I learned how to play—nervous or not (that certainly was a help for performances later). He was a wonderful teacher, giving me regular professional training, in many ways similar to the rigorous coaching an athlete receives in training for the Olympics. This was the beginning of my lifelong fascination with the liquid, moving sound of the flute as well as with the form and beauty of music.

As a soprano voice of the woodwinds, the flute often carries the melody. It can play very fast or be tender and warm, even whining and demanding. I try to express all these feelings, though it might take a lot of practice to do this. When I am not teaching myself I am teaching students. Ever since I was thirteen I have been teaching privately or in schools here or abroad—recently in China. American schools where I've taught include the Eastman School of Music, from which I also earned my bachelor of music degree, Yale, Boston University, and the Berkshire Music Center. I also play solos with orchestras and solo recitals. Soon I will play in Colorado where my daughter goes to college. Afterward we might go mountain climbing, though she is much better at that than I.

When away from my daughter, I like to spend time with friends, go to plays, concerts, antique shops, museums, and libraries. I have been a library user since I was a child and I have noticed that librarians seem to have an organized way of dealing with life, which I admire. In a library I get two feelings at once: that I want to read everything in sight and that I can never read enough.

From all my reading and my experience, it seems to me that the flute goes on forever. The ancient Greeks had entire orchestras of flutes, though the instrument was somewhat different then. The modern flute was developed in the nineteenth century by Theobald Boehm, who invented the key system in use today. Underneath one of the keys there is a cork about a quarter-inch thick. One time during a Boston Symphony concert, this cork fell out as I was playing a solo passage in Mendelssohn's *Italian* Symphony. It is fast music and, with the cork missing, many notes that I played sounded completely wrong, but luckily the conductor, Charles Munch, had a sense of humor. While I was cringing in embarrassment, he was shaking with laughter because of the way it sounded and because he had seen that cork rolling on the floor.

JANE COCHRAN

Oboe and English Horn, New York City Ballet Orchestra

The curious thing about the oboe is that it's both flexible and inflexible. It can be loud or soft, and tonally it can be bright or dark. Yet it has the least ability to change its pitch, and for this reason all of the other instruments tune to it. Because it takes very little breath to produce the oboe's sound, it is possible to play an extended melodic line without interrupting to take another breath. For this reason composers tend to give it long soulful solos like the one in Benjamin Britten's *Young Person's Guide to the Orchestra*.

I didn't know I was going to be an oboist until I was a student at the High School of Music and Art in New York. I was majoring in piano there and also had to study an orchestral instrument. The conductor put me in the woodwind section, where only the oboe and bassoon were left. I chose the oboe.

Usually someone starts woodwind study around thirteen years of age, much later than with the strings, because it requires strength in breathing. And among the woodwinds, the oboe demands the greatest breath control since the opening in its double reed is so small. Because you have to release the air so slowly through that tiny opening, it's like holding your breath, and beginning students sometimes get dizzy. Making my own reeds is the most intricate and really the most boring part of being an oboist.

While I was in college I studied with Harold Gomberg, who for many years was principal oboist in the New York Philharmonic. Later, I became a teacher at the Wisconsin Conservatory of Music. When I returned to New York, the musical life there was very active and I was able to play in several small orchestras. Then the New York City Ballet called me in when one of their oboists became sick. Because I'd had no rehearsal, I had to sight-read the whole program: Tchaikovsky's Third Suite and Stravinsky's *Firebird*. It was very frightening, but having gotten through this performance, I don't suffer anymore from stage nerves. After that first fill-in appearance, I became the regular substitute for the New York City Ballet Orchestra, and when an opening for an oboist came a couple of years later, I was hired without an audition.

As second oboist I also play all of the English horn parts, and in fact I have a special affinity for this instrument. Nobody really knows how it got its name; it's not English and it's not a horn. Longer than the oboe, it has a larger double reed and a

oboe

pear-shaped bell. Its tonal range lies between the oboe and the bassoon, and although it requires the same training and fingering as the oboe, controlling its dynamics and tone is more difficult. And of course it's more exposed in the orchestra because there's only one English horn as against three oboes. For a number of years I've played the English horn at the Casals Festival in Puerto Rico. It's one of the easiest orchestras to play in because the musicians are so extraordinarily good. They're chosen by reputation rather than by audition.

But whether with the Casals Festival Orchestra or here with the New York City Ballet, I'm playing some of the greatest repertoire ever written, and with the ballet I have the additional excitement of being associated with Mr. Balanchine's choreography.

English horn

MICHELE ZUKOVSKY

Co-Principal Clarinet, Los Angeles Philharmonic

Sometimes when people pack their suitcases for a trip they forget something. Once in a while when I get to the concert hall and open my clarinet case, I find that I've forgotten to put in one of the parts–there are five altogether. When I see that empty space, I think, "Oh no, now I have to borrow again." So far I haven't had to borrow from my father.

It's not unusual for two people in the same family to play the same instrument, but in our family my father and I both play the clarinet in the same orchestra. It works out fine, except that we have the same sense of humor and laugh at the same things. So if we both crack up at once when we have to play at the same time, no sound comes out. But luckily the conductor understands.

When I was little, I used to hear my father practicing and I would listen to him teaching his students. Soon I was studying with him, too, loving the clarinet's "woodsy" timbre and pure tone. Producing that pure tone is one of the most difficult things to do. You have to be able to hear it and that comes from listening to other fine players, and from having good instruction.

Even though I had both these experiences, listening and good instruction, from the time I was very young, my family and I never had any idea I'd become a professional clarinetist. But then, when I was eighteen I took my first and only audition. It was for assistant principal clarinet with the Los Angeles Philharmonic, and I was extremely

nervous, but less nervous than if I'd been older and more aware of the circumstances. There were about fifty other clarinetists auditioning. Nowadays there would be twice that many, since there are so many more fine clarinetists. I know because I've taught some of them.

When I'm not busy with teaching or with practicing or with making my reeds, I like to do things outdoors--like bike riding and camping with my husband, who is a clarinetist, too. The sounds of the woods appeal to me as much as the music of the orchestra.

I can still remember my first performance with the orchestra–the excitement of hearing those sounds all around me, large sounds, and being part of it. Understanding the music and bringing it across to the audience, communicating with an enormous audience, gives me a special feeling–the feeling of being lifted up out of the ordinary everyday things and of becoming part of something very special.

JOHN BRUCE YEH

Bass Clarinet, Chicago Symphony Orchestra

Because the bass clarinet doesn't get as much attention as the clarinet, a bass clarinetist has to have some sort of spark to start him off. For me, it was the American Youth Symphony; it laid the foundation for my orchestral career. Although I had started to study the clarinet when I was quite young, when I entered high school I tried the bass clarinet in the orchestra and really liked it. Then when I was with the American Youth Symphony, I went back to the clarinet. But the bass clarinetist quit when we were going to perform the Khachaturian Piano Concerto, which has one of the biggest bass clarinet parts ever written. The conductor, Mehli Mehta, who is Zubin Mehta's father and was the head of the conducting department at UCLA, asked the clarinetists, "Who'll play?" "I will," I said, "if you get me a good instrument." It was my first experience playing a big solo in an orchestra, and it gave me such great pleasure.

It's uncommon to find a clarinetist who's really interested in playing the bass clarinet, but for me it has always come very naturally. Big people generally find the bass clarinet easier to play than small people do because of the instrument's size and weight, and because it takes a lot more air than the clarinet. Some people say, "I'd rather not bother with something that's this large," and very few music schools offer a bass clarinet major. Juilliard is one that does, and I think that's because Joe Allard is there. He was the bass clarinetist in the NBC Symphony with Toscanini and is a master of many instruments. He taught me both bass clarinet and clarinet. Before that I had studied with Gary Gray at Aspen and at UCLA, where I had been a pre-med student before I decided that I really wanted to study music instead of medicine.

I guess the person who's had the greatest musical influence in my life, the one who's been my model, my mentor, my inspiration, is Harold Wright, principal clarinetist with the Boston Symphony Orchestra. I played for him when I auditioned for Tanglewood. I was dazed, in a stupor. Here was this man whose records I'd been listening to, whom I idolized, who represented for me the epitome of clarinet playing–he was going to listen to me! Studying with him that summer at Tanglewood was one of the great experiences of my life.

A couple of years later I auditioned for the Chicago Symphony Orchestra. To prepare for it I practiced five hours

a day for a month and kept in physical shape by jogging. It was a double audition for bass clarinet and clarinet, because to get the position I had to be able to play clarinet as well. Of course the practicing has continued since I joined the orchestra, but when you've worked so hard, not only in practice but in rehearsal, too, there's a personal pleasure, a satisfaction, that comes to you when you play well in the concert. I think it's the greatest thing to have achieved something I love to do, and at the same time to be able to make a living at it. In addition to playing in the orchestra, I'm also a founding member of the Chicago New Music Ensemble. So much of the bass clarinet repertoire is in ensemble music, and this gives me the opportunity to play it.

Probably my natural feeling for the bass clarinet is very much a matter of being in psychological agreement with the instrument. It has any number of moods: happy, melancholy, playful, funny. I love its dark, rich, fundamental color–the way it can sit at the bottom of a chord and really anchor everything. Unfortunately it has the reputation of being a background instrument, but actually it has a really flexible sound. Vincent Abato of the Metropolitan Opera Orchestra, a great bass clarinetist, once said to me, "Son," he said, "this is a solo instrument. Never forget that." I haven't.

BERNARD GARFIELD

Principal Bassoon, Philadelphia Orchestra

When I entered the High School of Music and Art, one of the teachers said, "Let me see your fingers and your teeth." I didn't know what that was all about until he exclaimed, "You can play the bassoon." That was fine with me because my brother had told me that when the conductor asked me, I should say I wanted to play horn or bassoon because those instruments are always needed. But the truth is, my fingers are too short, I have an overbite, and not enough lip for the bassoon. Even though I had to work extra hard because of these limitations, I wasn't sorry. I soon came to love the sound of the bassoon—its poignant expressiveness. The three-and-a-half octave range makes it possible to play very low, for the grandfather's part in Prokofiev's *Peter and the Wolf*, and very high, as in Stravinsky's *Rite of Spring* or Ravel's *Bolero*. *The Sorcerer's Apprentice* by Dukas shows how effectively it can bounce around from high to low.

Although I had been playing in amateur orchestras while I was going to school, being principal bassoonist under Koussevitsky in the student orchestra at Tanglewood was very special. Later I was with the New York City Ballet Orchestra for seven years, and then came to the Philadelphia twenty-two years ago. It's a busy life; we have four rehearsals and four concerts a week, two hundred concerts a year. I teach eleven hours a week at Temple University and Curtis Institute, and try to find time to compose music that features the bassoon (my master's degree at Columbia University was in musical composition).

Too much time is spent making reeds. It takes an hour to an hour and a half to make one, but I need 100 to 125 a year in order to cull out the 10 or so that play well. Unfortunately, you can't predict how well one will play while you're making it. The last few scrapings of the cane determine the sound. Bassoonists and other woodwind players will tell you that their mood depends on how well their reed is playing—when the reed is bad, everything is bad. A sympathetic friend once made me a huge reed. It's comforting to know there are people who understand.

Actually, the rest of the instrument requires some mechanical skill, too. Once, just before I was to play Copland's *Appalachian Spring* with Leonard Bernstein conducting, a piece of cork fell out of one of the levers. I had to repair it with glue instead of resin, and the glue was giving me trouble. I was really nervous because at one point in this piece the bassoon plays one note all alone. But the lever worked, the note sang, and everything was fine.

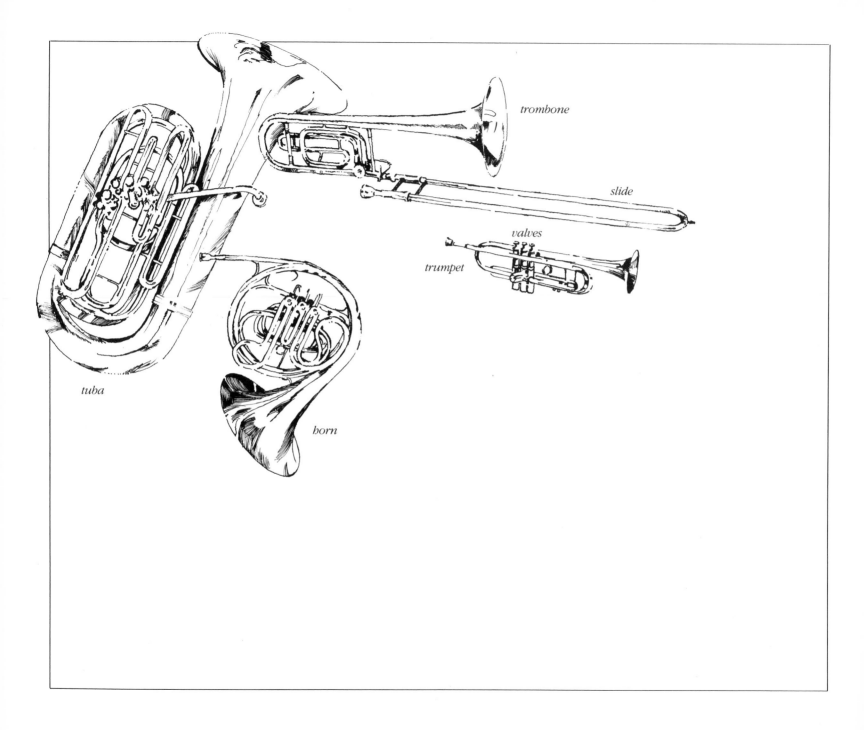

trombone

slide

valves

trumpet

tuba

horn

BRASS

The brass instruments work on the same vibrating column of air principle as the woodwinds. But instead of blowing through a reed (or across the mouth hole of the flute), the brass player uses his lips like a reed, varying their tension and blowing into the mouthpiece attached to the brass tubing. The length of the air column is changed on the trombone by moving the slide back and forth to seven different positions, and on the trumpet, horn, and tuba by pressing valves that direct the air through extra lengths of tubing.

Both the modern valved trumpet and horn were developed early in the last century but weren't fully accepted as orchestral instruments until the mid-nineteenth century. The trumpet bore is two-thirds cylindrical and one-third conical. The horn gradually broadens from its ¼-inch mouthpiece to the bell, which flares to fourteen inches. The tuba's mouthpiece is almost two inches wide and its bell, opening at the end of a very wide conical bore, is huge. In its present form the tuba was developed by Adolphe Sax in 1843. The much older trombone, about four hundred years old, has cylindrical tubing except as it broadens to form the bell.

MARK GOULD

Associate Principal Trumpet, Metropolitan Opera Orchestra

When I was in the eighth grade, I wanted to play in the school band, but I was given a test that showed I had no talent, and the conductor wouldn't give me an instrument. So I went out and rented a trumpet because I wanted very much to learn. I *did* learn, and I *did* play in the band, and in a year I was its best brass player.

Later, I studied music for four summers at the Interlochen Music Camp in Michigan, and I also learned a lot by playing in jazz bands. You have to be very flexible when you play jazz. Playing in the orchestra is different; it's hitting the target. If you miss a note there, everybody knows it because the trumpet is the most brilliant of the brass instruments. In a climax in a symphony the trumpet comes in above the whole orchestra. You're riding a wave on top of the orchestra. You're soaring. The trumpet is an aggressive instrument; you can't be timid with a trumpet. It's joyful, too. And of course it plays fanfares. It can play softer and louder than any instrument in the orchestra.

A couple of years ago a friend told me there was an opening for trumpet in the Metropolitan Opera Orchestra. So I thought, "Well, I'll audition." I was really surprised when I got the position. I was the only one in the orchestra who hadn't had a formal music background. And I hadn't ever been interested in opera; but now I really like it, especially Italian opera. It's lively, melodic; the trumpet can sing. Playing in the opera,

I've learned a lot about music, especially from the singers, because singing is the basis of all music.

But when I first got into the opera orchestra—now this is a horror story:

You see, in *Pagliacci* there's a trumpet call onstage. The musician who was supposed to play this couldn't, for some reason, and I was thrown in at the last minute. I hadn't rehearsed. So there I am, dressed in a leotard, ballet shoes, and a hat. They take away my glasses; I can't see a thing. I'm standing backstage, and I'm supposed to jump on a horse-drawn wagon. Nobody tells me to hold on, so when the wagon starts to move I almost fall off. The wagon has a cover. So then the cover comes off and I see the lead singers Richard Tucker and Anna Moffo laughing at me. Then they start singing. I get off the wagon and walk to the middle of the stage. It's dark. I'm supposed to go with a cue from a backstage conductor. The curtain is still closed. The orchestra plays the prelude. The audience applauds. My cue comes during the applause (it's supposed to come after). I start to play. A man in the cast screams at me to stop. I stop. Then the conductor signals for me to start again. There's a bass drum part played by a singer onstage. He gets it all wrong. I'm in a state of shock. The chorus comes on and I almost get trampled. What a night. It was the worst thing that ever happened to me.

But I'm still playing and I guess I always will, because, for me, music is magic.

CHARLES KAVALOVSKI

Principal Horn, Boston Symphony Orchestra

Although the horn is one of the most complicated-looking instruments in the orchestra, its ancestor was very simple, consisting only of a ram's horn with its top cut off so that the lips could be placed against the opening and "buzzed." Later, the Greeks and Romans made curved horns of wood and metal. About five hundred years ago, a horn was developed in Germany that was used for the hunt because it could be heard over long distances. A slightly different instrument evolved in France, where it was called *cor-de-chasse*, which means "horn of the chase" or "hunting horn." As the horn developed historically, more and more tubing was added in the shape of loops so that if you were to lay out all the tubing in a modern horn end-to-end, it would stretch about thirty feet!

Because of its long history in the hunt, the horn was thought of as an outdoor instrument and wasn't used in the orchestra until the eighteenth century. The early form of the horn was able to play only a few, widely spaced notes, so the music written for it was very simple. Later, valves were added and the horn can now play complete chromatic scales, like the piano.

Besides having the widest range of notes of all the brasses, the horn has, I think, the greatest range of moods, and is the closest to the human voice in its ability to express emotion. Its dark, mysterious sound has fascinated composers for over two hundred

years. Although it is used often for romantic, lyrical music, it is equally suited to the rollicking hunting music of its early days.

Because the horn's tubing is so long, the pitch of the instrument is easily affected by changes in temperature, humidity, and altitude. Sometimes at our outdoor concerts at Tanglewood, the temperature onstage can be as low as fifty degrees, and I find I have to keep my horn inside my tux jacket when I'm not playing so that it doesn't get impossibly out of tune. During my first year in the Boston Symphony I went on a tour to South America. We played in Bogota, Columbia, at an elevation of ten thousand feet, and I remember how differently the horn played there because the air was so much thinner at that altitude. I found I had to take a lot more breaths when I was playing, too. There were even oxygen tanks backstage in case any of us should feel faint.

In spite of occasional problems of that sort, traveling is one of the most fascinating aspects of my job. The orchestra recently went to China to present concerts in Peking and Shanghai and to work with the musicians there. Western music is relatively new to the Chinese, and they were very eager to learn from us and to help us appreciate their culture better. I think trips like this go a long way toward promoting world peace and understanding.

Teaching here in Boston is very much a part of my career, too. You might say I began horn teaching with myself, because I am largely self-taught. I started the study of the horn in high school and continued during college and graduate school, where I earned a Ph.D. in physics. It took a lot of self-discipline to sit down to practice the horn two or three hours every day on top of my studies without a teacher to keep after me. I think you can learn to do just about anything, though, if you want to badly enough.

It was after I had been a physics professor for about seven years that I began to think about becoming a professional musician. I was teaching in Washington at the time and decided to give the music business a try to see how I liked it. There was an opening in the Denver Symphony so I flew down to audition for it. Playing an audition at six thousand feet above sea level in that dry, western air was quite an experience, but everything turned out well and I got the job. Later that year I auditioned for solo horn with the Boston Symphony Orchestra and was fortunate enough to win a position with one of the finest orchestras in the world. I guess I'm pretty lucky to have had the chance to try two very different careers. Although I enjoy life as a symphony musician so far, I know that if I ever get bored with it, there are lots of other things out there for me to try!

JAY FRIEDMAN

Principal Trombone, Chicago Symphony Orchestra

A very long time ago the name for the trombone was sackbut, a name that probably came from two French words meaning pull-push. It was that pull-push, moving the slide back and forth to get the right tone, that was the hardest part for me to learn. I was nine when I started playing a musical instrument. It was a band instrument called the baritone, but by the time I graduated from high school I had decided I wanted to be a professional musician. That's when I took up the trombone and studied with a member of the Chicago Symphony Orchestra.

I had been playing with the Civic Orchestra, a training orchestra in Chicago, for four years when I got a job with the Florida Symphony. Two years later my teacher, who was in the Chicago Symphony, told me about a trombone opening there and I got that job. My first concert with the Chicago Symphony Orchestra was really exciting, although I wasn't nervous because by that time I had had quite a bit of experience and I knew I could do it. But I wasn't so sure of myself another time when I dropped a mute in a very quiet part of a piece and it fell on the floor–clang! You should have seen the conductor.

The trombone can play either very soft–that's when I use the mute–or loud; it can be mysterious or threatening, ponderous or melodious. Composers often bring out its religious, noble quality. And among the brass instruments it's the one that blends most perfectly with more of itself; that is, two or more trombones playing together produce a

better integrated sound than a grouping of trumpets, horns, or tubas. The thing I like about the trombone is that even though the slide requires that the player have a really fine sense of pitch (since he has only his ear to guide him in moving the slide to the exact position to produce the right tone), it also makes it possible to play perfectly in tune because you can make such fine adjustments to the length of the air column.

I know that I became a musician because my father's side of the family was very musical and there was always a good deal of music around the house, but I don't know why I became so fascinated with horses. Because I grew up in the city, it wasn't possible to keep a horse, or even to do much riding, but I loved horses. I had been a professional musician for fifteen years when I moved to the country and apprenticed myself to a really good horse trainer. After many years I was ready to train my own horses. My wife and I started with a two-stall barn and a few acres of land, and this spring we added a new ten-stall barn and an arena. Horse training and trombone playing may seem like a strange combination of careers, but I love them both.

HERBERT WEKSELBLATT

Tuba, Metropolitan Opera Orchestra

At the Metropolitan Opera House, or the Met as it is commonly called, we musicians sit in the orchestra pit, which is in front of and below the stage and about six feet below the first row of seats in the theater. Sometimes when a world-renowned soprano comes out for her first curtain call after a performance, her admirers in the top balcony seats create a snowfall of shredded paper. It settles on the stage and on us in the pit. It also begins to fill up the upward-facing bell of my tuba if I don't turn it upside down quickly enough

Before I took my place in the Met pit nineteen years ago, I had been playing on television, in recording studios, and with the New York City Ballet as well as the New York City Opera Orchestras. I started to study the tuba when I was thirteen. My mother was eager for me to take music lessons, but it would have been very costly to buy an instrument. A free tuba solved the problem. It happened because the conductor at the local music school needed a tuba player so desperately that he told my mother he would loan an instrument to me if I would play it in his band. At first I was unhappy because I wanted to play the saxophone, but when I found that I could actually produce a sound on the huge tuba, I really got excited about it. My lessons cost only thirty-five cents because it was during the Depression, the school was in a poor neighborhood, and the conductor *really* needed a tuba player.

The man who invented the instrument I originally wanted to play also developed the tuba as we know it today. His name was Adolphe Sax and he is responsible for a whole family of brass instruments called saxhorns that he patented in the mid-nineteenth century. Of all the saxhorns, and in fact of all the brass instruments, the tuba has both the greatest length of tubing and the largest bell. It is also the heaviest and the deepest sounding. The composer Wagner used that sound in *Siegfried*. In that opera Siegfried, the hero, must slay the dragon and that huge beast is described by the tuba–very deep and threatening. But in Prokofiev's *Love for Three Oranges*, the tuba plays a happy tune as a fat cook comes on stage.

Of course I can't see the stage from where I sit in the pit–usually in the same line as the trumpets and trombones. We listen very carefully to each other so as not to play too loud or too soft and we like working together that way. But there is one big problem with being the tuba player in the Met orchestra–sitting in front of the percussion section. When the conductor raises his hands to signal for a big sound, the bass drum, timpani, and cymbals can be unbelievably loud.

I've gotten used to that, but not to the excitement that comes with the opening of each performance. I know the opera is about to start when I see the chandeliers begin to rise to the ceiling and the house lights get dimmer and dimmer. Finally the theater is completely dark except for the lights on our music stands. There is silence, then a sudden burst of applause as the conductor strides to the podium. He bows to the audience, then to the orchestra. He raises his baton, holds it there until the audience is quiet. Then the downbeat–and the music begins.

PERCUSSION

Some kind of drum was probably our first instrument–the kettle drum, or timpano (from the Latin *timpanum* meaning "a vibrating membrane"), is known to have been used in the time of David and Solomon. But the pedal-tuned timpani weren't developed until 1872 in Dresden. Today's kettles are still made of copper (although some are fiberglass) and the heads are calfskin or plastic. Striking the head with balls of felt on the ends of hickory sticks causes the air in the kettle to vibrate and so produces the sound. The pitch is changed by tightening or loosening the tension on the head. Unlike the other drums, the timpani can be tuned to a definite pitch. At least two and often three, four, or more timpani are used in the orchestra depending on the demands of the music.

Only one bass drum is required. It is very large–thirty-six or more inches wide and at least seventeen inches deep. Struck with a felt-headed stick, it produces a very low, powerful sound of indefinite pitch. Until the nineteenth century it was called the "Turkish drum" and is known to have been played in a Turkish band in the early sixteenth century. Some form of the snare drum is thought to have been in use from the twelfth century on. In its modern form it is usually fourteen inches across and at least six inches deep and has a number of wires stretched across the lower head that make its sizzling sound. The drum produces a brilliant sound when struck with wooden sticks.

The clanging sound of the cymbals was heard as long ago as the seventh century. In their present form, they are large brass discs held vertically and struck together. Striking a

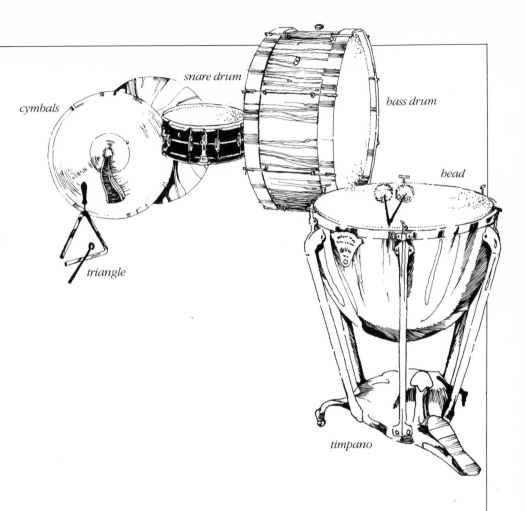

cymbals

snare drum

bass drum

head

triangle

timpano

triangle with a small metal stick produces a tinkling sound. Now made of a metal rod bent into a triangle, the triangle wasn't always triangular. When it first appeared in the fifteenth century, it sometimes had the shape of a medieval stirrup. In addition to the timpani, drums, cymbals, and triangle, there are a number of other percussion instruments that are used to achieve particular effects.

CLOYD DUFF

Principal Timpani, Cleveland Orchestra

My mother's pots and pans were my first drums. When I was four years old I took them out of the kitchen cabinets, spread them out on the floor, and hit them with a stick. My parents didn't mind the clatter and two years later they gave me a set of drums for Christmas. From that time on I never stopped playing drums of one kind or another. I continued with the snare drums and xylophone in my elementary and high school orchestras, but then when I was a senior in high school, I heard my first symphony orchestra concert. It was the Detroit Symphony Orchestra and as I listened I decided, "I really like the timpani." Just about that time my high school got its first set of timpani. Who would play them? After all my years of handling the snare drumsticks I knew I could, and I did.

That summer I won a scholarship to the Ohio Band Camp and studied timpani and percussion with Ned Albright. Some members of the Cleveland Orchestra were also teaching at the camp and they suggested that I apply to the Curtis Institute of Music in Philadelphia. So I auditioned and was given a scholarship to study with Oscar Schwar, timpanist of the Philadelphia Orchestra. After graduation I joined the Indianapolis Symphony as principal timpanist. I spent the summers touring with the All American Youth Orchestra under Leopold Stokowski, or playing in the Robin Hood Dell Concerts in Philadelphia. In 1942, when I was twenty-six years old, I joined the Cleveland Orchestra

and found myself playing with the same people who had encouraged me that summer at band camp eight years earlier. I can't help feeling pleased that I started with the Cleveland Orchestra under Arturo Rodzinski and have remained with it through the directorships of Leinsdorf, Szell, and Maazel. It's been a wonderful experience to grow with the orchestra over these thirty-eight years. During a concert I set a playing standard for myself and try to better it. I also play to meet the standards that my colleagues and the conductor expect of me.

While the timpani, or kettle drums as they're also called, are considered members of the percussion group, they are the only drums that can be tuned to different pitches. I think of them as tonal rather than percussion instruments and I play them that way; the sound should have the quality of a pizzicato cello. I have to tune my drums (usually three, but sometimes as many as seven) while the orchestra is playing and count my rests in the music all the while so that I will come in at the right time. It takes lots of experience and an excellent sense of pitch to be able to do this. When I'm tuning I very lightly tap the drumheads, which are stretched over the copper "kettles." The plastic heads that I now use most of the time are very strong and this is good because often during a piece I am required to beat them quite hard. I also sometimes use calfskin heads but they are much more expensive than plastic, don't last as long, and sometimes break during a rehearsal or concert. Until recently, calfskin heads were the only ones available.

I think the timpani have one of the most interesting histories of all the orchestral instruments. During the Crusades they were brought to Europe from Asia Minor and, along with trumpets, were played on horseback by attacking armies. Then the Western European royalty claimed them for themselves and it was forbidden for kettle drums or trumpets to be used for anyone but royalty. The king's musicians played their instruments on horseback to herald the approach of royalty. But then composers were attracted to the sound of the kettle drums and trumpets and brought them right out of the stable, so to speak, and into the concert halls. Today the kettle drums, as well as trumpets, are still a part of the pageantry of royalty, in parades at Buckingham Palace in London and the famous tattoos of Edinburgh, Scotland. But the timpani, as they are usually called today, are primarily used as a prominent orchestral instrument.

ELDEN ("BUSTER") BAILEY

Percussion, New York Philharmonic

When I was four years old I was given a little toy drum, and I've been playing drums ever since. We lived in Portland, Maine, where there always seemed to be lots of parades, and my mother took me to all of them. I loved the sound of the drums, and when I was six years old I began taking drum lessons with an excellent teacher.

In elementary school I played in the Drum and Bugle Corps, and later in the high-school band. Our neighbor was a band master, and he taught me a great deal about music. After high school I studied at the New England Conservatory of Music, and then went into the Army, where I played drums in the band for three years. Then came more studying at the Juilliard School in New York. Now I teach there. While I was in my last year at Juilliard, I played in the Little Orchestra Society of New York. After graduation I joined the New York Philharmonic and I've been here ever since, thirty-one years.

Although the drum is one of the oldest instruments, it was one of the last to be used in symphonic music. I play the snare drum and the bass drum, but the snare drum is my favorite. When you hear a drumroll, sometimes that's the snare drum playing. Its name comes from the wire, or gut, strands called snares that are stretched across the bottom head and make that sizzling sound. The drumheads are made of calfskin or plastic, and the sticks are hickory or maple wood. But sometimes I don't use the wooden sticks. At the beginning of Ravel's *Bolero* the snare plays alone and starts very, very softly. I play that part

bass drum

with English pennies! Then as it gets a little louder, I switch to number-fifteen knitting needles that my wife gave me; I strike the drum with the heads of the needles. And then finally, I use the wooden sticks. I have many, many sticks because I need different sizes and weights to make different sounds.

In addition to the drums I also play the cymbals, triangle, gong, chimes, tambourine, and xylophone, all members of the percussion family and each with its own distinctive sound. Often the snare drumrolls remind me of the circus.

Sometimes there was circus music in the parades I went to when I was a child. All my life I've loved the circus, and for the past eighteen years I've been collecting circus things. I have models of circus wagons, about 350 miniature elephants, 200 books about the circus, movies and photographs, and diaries and programs–some of them 100 years old. The collection has grown so large that we have a special room for it in our house. When my nieces and nephews come to visit, they like to sleep in the "circus room." Recordings of circus music are among the things I care most about in my collection, and when I have the time, I love to play in circus bands. One season when the drummer with the Ringling Brothers and Barnum & Bailey Circus was very sick with flu, I took his place. That's when I was able to play plenty of drumrolls.

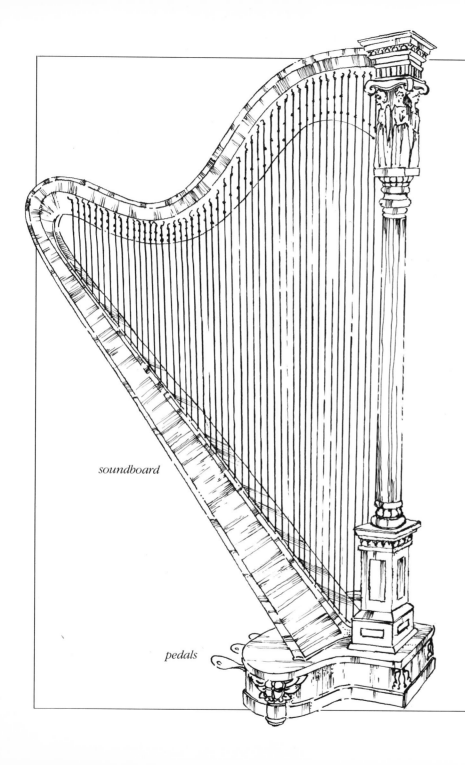

soundboard

pedals

THE HARP

Although its ancestors are five thousand years old, the harp as we know it now was developed early in the nineteenth century. Its forty-seven strings can produce many more than forty-seven tones when they are plucked because there are seven pedals that the harpist can use to shorten or lengthen the strings and so change their pitches. The wooden soundboard, the part that slants up and back from the base and to which the strings are attached, amplifies the sound of the strings.

ANN HOBSON

Associate Principal Harp, Boston Symphony Orchestra

Most people commute to work, but usually over relatively short distances. Being able to play second harp in the Pittsburgh Symphony meant so much to me that I was more than willing to commute over one hundred miles from where I was studying at the Cleveland Institute of Music. After a year with the Pittsburgh I moved to the National Symphony in Washington, and from there to Boston. That was eleven years ago.

In the orchestra the harp seldom plays a melody. It is usually an accompanying instrument, providing richness of sound with chords, arpeggios, and glissandos. The French Impressionist composers Debussy and Ravel often used it to provide color. For instance, in Debussy's *La Mer* the harp glissandos suggest the waves of the sea. Ginestera, a contemporary composer, uses it as a percussion instrument, requiring the harpist to bang on the soundboard. That's very different from the way it was played long, long ago. It looked different then, too–like the bow that's used to shoot an arrow. The Bible tells about David playing the harp.

The modern harp, which has pedals so that it can play in all keys, was developed about 150 years ago. Those pedals got me in trouble once. At a concert in high school I tuned my harp after the intermission without realizing that one of the pedals had been held down. As a result, I tuned a half tone off. When I discovered this, I just didn't play at all in that part of the concert. The conductor looked so puzzled. Afterward, when I explained what had happened, he was very kind and understanding.

But that wasn't as upsetting as the time I was on tour with the National Symphony in Italy. There was no harp part in the first piece on the program, but there was in the second composition. The backstage guard didn't understand that I was a member of the orchestra since I hadn't been with them for the first piece. I tried to explain, but I don't speak much Italian and he didn't understand English, so he wouldn't unlock the door and let me go onstage. Well, I ran as fast as I could to the other side of the stage where the door was unlocked and made it just in time to walk on with the conductor.

celesta

harpsichord

piano

KEYBOARD INSTRUMENTS

Invented in 1709 by Cristofori, the original piano had a shorter tonal range than the seven and one-quarter octaves of today's instrument. A string instrument, its sound is produced when the strings are struck by hammers that are controlled by the eighty-eight keys–fifty-two white and thirty-six black–of the keyboard. There are also three pedals–the loud, the soft, and the sustaining–that affect the sound.

Lacking the dynamic range of the piano, the harpsichord is about three hundred years older and usually has two keyboards. Its twangy sound results from the plucking instead of the striking of the strings. However, it is the striking mechanism that produces the celesta's sound. The hammers strike metal bars rather than strings, producing pure tones something like the sound of soft chimes. A young instrument, the celesta was invented by the Frenchman Auguste Mustel in 1886.

The oldest of all these keyboard instruments, the organ can be traced in its early form back to 250 B.C. The contemporary concert hall organ can vary in size and have as many as several thousand pipes, which are grouped in sets called stops. In its smaller version, it looks something like an upright piano but with more than one keyboard. The sound of the organ is produced when air is forced through its pipes. This process is controlled by the keyboards, sometimes five to seven, one of which, the pedal board, is played by the feet. Although we usually associate the organ with church music, many orchestras play symphonic music incorporating it.

JOELA JONES

Principal Keyboard, Cleveland Orchestra

One of the first piano pieces children learn to play is an old French folk tune. We call it "Twinkle, Twinkle, Little Star." Over the years a number of composers have written variations on this tune, and when I was eleven I met one of these composers. His name was Ernst von Dohnanyi and, in addition to being a composer, he was a magnificent pianist. It was a great honor for me to attend his piano master classes–to hear fine pianists and to play for him. As a young man he had studied composition with Brahms, but when I met Dohnanyi he was an old man. At the beginning of each piano class Dohnanyi would greet me and shake my hand. And I would think, "I'm shaking the hand that shook the hand of Brahms." That's when I knew I wanted to become a professional pianist.

My mother was my first music teacher. She began giving me piano lessons when I was five and I suppose because I loved music it was easy for me to learn; I even enjoyed practicing. When I was thirteen we moved from Florida to Rochester, New York, and I studied on a scholarship at the Eastman School of Music. It was there that I met Arthur Fiedler, who invited me to appear as a soloist with the Boston Pops Orchestra. After returning to Florida to finish my high school education, I went to Cleveland to continue my piano studies at the Cleveland Institute of Music and to take non-music courses at Case Western Reserve University. I received both my bachelor and master of music degrees by the time I was twenty.

piano

Perhaps twenty is young to be finishing school, but I was eager to earn my degrees so that, after graduation, I could continue my performance career. At that time there were two keyboardists with the Cleveland Orchestra, both of whom were also assistant conductors of the orchestra. One of them was scheduled to conduct a Cleveland Orchestra concert of Stravinsky's *Petrouchka*, which has a prominent piano part. The other keyboardist was out of town so I was asked to substitute for him and to play the piano part. (I had performed once before with the Cleveland Orchestra, as a guest soloist, while I was still at the Cleveland Institute of Music. I played the Russell Smith Piano Concerto –brilliant, long, and very difficult. Performing it with the renowned George Szell conducting was a thrilling experience.) About a year after the *Petrouchka* performance I was asked to join the Cleveland Orchestra, and at that time I concentrated more on the organ and the harpsichord, instruments a keyboard performer has to play in addition to the celesta and the piano.

Of these four instruments, the celesta is the youngest–about one hundred years old. Its keyboard is about half the size of the piano's and so is its tonal range, rising four octaves from middle C. Most people know its sound from "The Dance of the Sugar Plum Fairy" in Tchaikovsky's *Nutcracker* Suite.

The harpsichord, which is five hundred years older than the celesta, appeared at the beginning of the fifteenth century. A great amount of music was written for the instrument some 250 years ago–I especially enjoy playing J.S. Bach's music–and recently contemporary composers have begun composing music for the harpsichord again.

In addition to my duties as keyboardist with the orchestra, I am rehearsal accompanist for the Cleveland Orchestra Chorus and for the vocal artists who are to appear as soloists. The piano is very well-suited for this because it can suggest the sound of the whole orchestra. Pianoforte, the full name for the piano, means soft-loud. It was given that name by its inventor about 250 years ago because the keyboard instruments of that time, the harpsichord and the clavichord, lacked any significant dynamic range. In addition to its great dynamic range, the piano with its eighty-eight keys has the widest tonal range of all the instruments except the organ.

Besides playing orchestral piano parts, I frequently appear as concerto soloist with the orchestra, and I also perform with various chamber music groups. Many orchestra members enjoy playing chamber music, which is music written for a small group of performers. My husband, Richard Weiss, who is the first assistant principal cellist in the orchestra, and I are members of a chamber music group called New Cleveland Consort. All great orchestras are comparable to a large chamber music ensemble. I have tremendous respect for this orchestra; it's a privilege to be a member of it.

CONDUCTOR

There is a story told about Toscanini, the man considered by many to be the greatest conductor of this century. While talking at home with a friend about conducting, Toscanini picked up a baton to demonstrate a point. Catching sight of himself in a mirror, he began to laugh, threw down the baton, and said, "Isn't this a silly thing for a grown man to be doing?"

Because it is the most visible and dramatic of all the conductor's activities, as well as the ultimate test of his skill, his or her work with the baton draws most of our attention. But a lot of time and effort go into the preparation for the concert: selecting the program, studying scores, and rehearsing the orchestra.

In rehearsals and in the performance the conductor is telling the musicians how he or she wants them to play by beating time with the baton in one hand, by signaling with motions of the other hand, and even through facial expression. But the most important of these is the beat.

Conducting has not always been a separate function. In the eighteenth century the concertmaster shared the conducting duties with a harpsichordist, organist, or pianist who directed from the keyboard. It wasn't until the nineteenth century that the conductor acquired the separate and dominant role that we know today.

SERGIU COMISSIONA

Music Director, Baltimore Symphony Orchestra

One Sunday afternoon when I was five, I heard music coming from the street in front of our house. Looking out the window, I saw a procession going by. It was one of the gypsy bands of very primitive but gifted musicians–musicians of tremendous technical ability who performed in the streets of Bucharest, Romania, where we lived. I was enchanted with the sound and ran out to follow it. The rhythm and vigor of the gypsies' playing, their singing and dancing were irresistible to me and I followed them, fascinated. After a while the realization came to me that I didn't know where I was; I was lost, but I didn't care and I continued to follow until the procession turned into a park, where the music became the accompaniment to a joyful ceremony–a wedding, I think. Caught in the magic, I settled on the grass to watch and listen. And that's where my frantic parents found me. They had been searching everywhere for me. A scolding and a spanking ended the adventure, but not my love of music.

My parents understood; soon after that Sunday afternoon they took me to a concert. And then, responding to my excitement, they gave me a subscription to the Bucharest Philharmonic. It didn't matter that the seat was in the last row; it was the greatest gift my parents could give me. After each concert I couldn't wait for the next time–to be with music. And to watch the conductor.

It seems to me now that there was never a time when I didn't want to be a conductor. As

a child I would wave my arms to the music on the radio or recordings, never any doubt in my mind that I would someday be a conductor. I would close my eyes and see myself as a conductor, dreaming that the regular conductor becomes sick and I jump onstage from the last row in the hall and conduct the performance.

But it wasn't all dreaming. When I was fourteen my formal conducting training began. (I had already been studying music at the Bucharest Conservatory.) Edouard Linderberg of the German Scherchen school of conducting was my first teacher and my first god. He sensed that I was basically a lazy person and so he scheduled my lessons at 6:00 A.M.! I had to get up at 4:30 and if I was late I didn't get a lesson. Instead he would talk to me kindly about the human problems in the life of a conductor–the need for self-discipline. My second god was the Romanian Silvestri, who taught me how to fill the music: "Every note has a meaning."

Long before I began to study with Linderberg and then Silvestri, I had been a violin student and when I was eighteen was playing in the opera orchestra. Shortly before a performance the regular conductor became ill and suddenly my dream was coming true. I had only a couple of hours to prepare and was so tense I didn't know what was happening. But somehow it worked out and several years later I became the principal conductor of the Romanian State Ensemble and conducted everything from puppet shows to symphony concerts.

Having been a violinist was a great help in conducting because it had trained my ear to the string sound, which is so important in the orchestra. But a conductor really has to know the possibilities of each instrument: how long a phrase can it play, how loud and how soft, what are the intonation problems, how much preparation time does the player need–for instance, the string sounds as soon as the bow touches it, but the horn isn't

76

heard immediately to the player's blowing into the mouthpiece. I like to work with the musicians on these problems, but I especially want to help the young players develop their imagination so that they will find more and more enjoyment in music.

After a number of years with the Romanian State Ensemble I left Romania and conducted in Sweden and Ireland. I also helped form several orchestras in Israel and toured the United States with the Israel Chamber Orchestra. That tour led to invitations to guest-conduct the Philadelphia, Boston, and Chicago Symphony Orchestras and finally to the directorship of the Baltimore Symphony Orchestra. I'm also advisor to the American and the Houston Symphony Orchestras and take every opportunity to conduct opera in the United States and in Europe. A conductor's career is like the broom in *The Sorcerer's Apprentice*—once it gets started you can't stop it.

And it doesn't all take place on the podium. An enormous amount of time is spent planning schedules and programs, working with the principal players of each section and with guest soloists, and, of course, studying scores. Among these scores are those of contemporary composers, since the Baltimore Symphony commissions a new work every season. I'm very proud to have won the Columbia University 1979 Ditson Conductor's Award for contributing to the advancement of contemporary American music because I feel it's the conductor's duty to discover new things, to continue the Stokowski legacy by encouraging contemporary composers.

I also feel a commitment to help develop young American conductors. When I was starting my career in Europe I won second prize in the Besançon conductor's competition in France, but there was no comparable contest in America and young American conductors had to go to Europe to try to win this kind of recognition. That's why I've started the Baltimore Symphony sponsorship of a biannual Young Conductor's Competition. I think I have a good nose for detecting conducting talent. Ronald Braunstein, who was one of our contestants, has just recently gone on to win first prize in the Karajan competition in Berlin. The young conductor Isaiah Jackson is now associate conductor with Rochester and Murray Sidlin is the music director of the New Haven Symphony.

It's hard to say what the quality is that I sense in these beginning conductors, but it's more than technique. When I was thirty years old and conducting in Israel, I thought, "I'm a good conductor now, but my music doesn't sound like Comissiona; it sounds like other conductors. How will I make the transition from being a good conductor to being Comissiona?" Now I understand that it comes from living, that all of my life experiences—happy or sad, good or bad—are translated into my music, making it more warm, more complete, more my own.

GLOSSARY

ARPEGGIO: Notes of a chord played one after the other in rapid succession; from the Italian *arpeggiare*, "to play upon a harp."

BASS: The lowest or deepest part in a musical composition.

BELL: The outward-curving opening at the outer end of the woodwinds (with the exception of the flute) and the brass instruments.

BOWING PATTERN: The series of bow strokes chosen for the playing of a motive, a phrase, or a melody.

BOWING TECHNIQUE: The control of the bow on the strings.

CHROMATIC SCALE: The division of the octave into twelve half-tones.

CONCERTO: A musical composition in which a solo player performs in combination with the orchestra; from the Latin *concertare*, "to compete as brothers in arms."

CORK: A small piece of cork glued under the key levers of the woodwind instruments to act as bumpers that stop the keys from opening too far and also silence the mechanical sounds of the metal lever striking against the body of the instrument.

DYNAMICS: The loudness or softness of the sound.

ENSEMBLE MUSIC: Music written for a small group of performers, for instance, chamber music as opposed to orchestral music. Each performer has a separate part.

GLISSANDO: A rapid sliding over the strings of the harp.

MAJOR SCALE: A succession of notes arranged in whole and half steps, the half steps coming between the third and fourth notes and the seventh and eighth notes, and given a key name according to its first or "home" note. For instance, the scale of the key of C begins on C.

MELODY: A succession of single tones related by pitch and rhythm.

MINOR SCALE: There are several minor scales. The most commonly used is the harmonic minor, which has a half step between the second and third, fifth and sixth, and seventh and eighth notes. All of the minor scales have the half step between the second and third notes in common and all are named, as in the major scale, for the first note of the scale.

MOTIVE: A brief, but distinct, musical pattern.

OCTAVE: The eighth tone of the major or minor scale.

PHRASE: A single and complete musical thought.

PITCH: The location of a particular tone in relation to all the other musical tones. It is determined by the frequency of vibration of the sounding body, for example, the string or air column.

PIZZICATO: The plucking (rather than bowing) of a string.

REED: A single or double piece of cane that when blown through causes the air column in the instrument to vibrate.

SINGLE REED: A strip of cane that beats against the mouthpiece of the instrument (clarinet and bass clarinet).

DOUBLE REED: Two pieces of cane that are bound together and beat against each other (oboe, English horn, bassoon).

RESIN: A preparation made from the gum residue of turpentine after distillation. It is applied to the hair of the bow to give it the necessary bite on the strings. It is also used by the bassoon player in this book, although not necessarily by other bassoon players, to hold the cork on the key levers of his instrument.

SOPRANO: The high female voice or the highest pitched member in a family of instruments. For example, the violin of the strings.

TANGLEWOOD: The countryside summer home in Lenox, Massachusetts, of the Boston Symphony Orchestra, where the orchestra performs a full schedule of concerts. Young music students audition there to win the opportunity to study with members of the orchestra.

TENOR: The high male voice or an instrument whose tonal range lies close to the tenor voice.

TONAL QUALITY OR TIMBRE: The sound that gives an instrument its individual aural characteristic, so that when two instruments, the violin and the clarinet, for example, play the identical pitch, they are easily distinguished from each other.

TONE: A sound that has definite pitch. Musicians in the orchestra tune to the A, 440 vibrations per second.

TUNE: To bring to the desired pitch.

VALVE: A mechansim for increasing the length of the air column in the brass instruments by diverting the air stream into additional tubing. Invented about 1815 by Bluhmel in Silesia and Stölzel in Berlin for the trumpet and horn, it was later adapted by Adolphe Sax to create the saxhorns.